AMITABHA

A STORY OF

BUDDHIST THEOLOGY

AMITABHA

A STORY OF
BUDDHIST THEOLOGY

By
PAUL CARUS

GYAN

Published by

Gyan Publishing House
5, Ansari Road
Daryaganj, New Delhi-110002
Phone: 011-47034999, 9811692060
E-mail: books@gyanbooks.com

Distribution Network
gyanbooks.com
India, USA, Canada, UK, Australia

ISBN: 978-93-6433-210-1 (PB)
First Published, 1906

2nd Impression 2024

Printed at: Gyan Press, Delhi.

AMITABHA A STORY OF BUDDHIST THEOLOGY
Author: PAUL CARUS

AMITABHA

A STORY OF

BUDDHIST THEOLOGY

BY

PAUL CARUS

MANIFESTING HIMSELF EVERYWHERE THE BUDDHA OF BLISS IS INFINITE, BOUNDLESS, LIMITLESS, UNCEASING, AND OF A SPIRITUAL NATURE.

AÇVAGHOSHA IN HIS "DISCOURSE ON THE AWAKENING OF FAITH."

CHICAGO
THE OPEN COURT PUBLISHING COMPANY
LONDON AGENTS
KEGAN PAUL, TRENCH, TRÜBNER & CO., LTD.
1906

THE ORDINATION.[1]

SOON after the time of Açoka, the great Buddhist emperor of the third century before Christ, India became the theater of protracted invasions and wars. Vigorous tribes from the North conquered the region of the upper Panjab and founded several states, among which the Kingdom of Gandhâra became most powerful. Despoliations, epidemics, and famines visited the valley of the Ganges, but all these tribulations passed over the religious institutions without doing them any harm. Kings lost their crowns and the wealthy their riches, but the monks chanted their hymns in the selfsame way. Thus the storm breaks down mighty trees, but only bends the yielding reed.

By the virtues, especially the equanimity and thoughtfulness, of the Buddhist priests, the conquerors in their turn were spiritually conquered by the conquered, and they embraced the religion of enlightenment. They recognised the four noble truths taught by the Tathâgata: (1) the prevalence of suffering which is always in evidence in this world; (2) the origin of suffering as rising from the desire of selfishness; (3) the possibility of emancipation from suffering by abandoning all selfish clinging; and (4) the way of salvation from evil by walking in the noble eightfold path of moral conduct, consisting in right comprehension, right aspiration, right speech, right conduct, right living, right endeavor, right discipline, and the attainment of the right bliss.

When the kingdom of Gandhâra had been firmly established, commerce and trade began to thrive more than ever, while the vihâras, or Buddhist monasteries, continued to be the home of religious exercises, offering an asylum to those who sought retirement from the turmoil of the world for the sake of finding peace of soul.

It was in one of these vihâras in the mountains near Purushaputra, the present Peshawur, that Charaka, a descendant of the Northern invaders, had decided to join the brotherhood.[2] He was as yet little acquainted with the spirit and purpose of the institution; but being very serious and devoutly religious, the youth had decided, for the sake of attaining perfect enlightenment, to give up everything dear to him, his parents, his home, his brilliant prospect of a promising future, and the love that was secretly budding in his heart.

The vihâra which Charaka entered was excavated in the solid rock of an idyllic gorge. A streamlet gurgled by, affording to the hermits abundance of fresh water, and the monks could easily sustain their lives by the gifts of the villagers who lived near by, to which they added the harvest of fruit and vegetables which grew near their cave dwellings. In the midst of their small cells was a large chaitya, a hall or church, in which they assembled for daily services, for sermons, meditations, and other pious exercises.

The chaitya, like the cells, was hewn out of the living rock; a row of massive columns on either side divided the hall into a central nave and two aisles.

The ornaments that covered the faces of the rocky walls, though the product of home talent, being made by the untrained hands of monk artists, did not lack a certain refinement and loftiness. The pictures exhibited scenes from the life of Buddha, his birth, his deeds, his miracles, illustrations of his parables, his sermons, and his final entry into Nirvâna.

A procession of monks, preceded by a leader who swung a censer, filed in through the large portal of the chaitya. Two by two they moved along the aisles and solemnly circumambulated the dagoba, standing at the end of the nave in the apse of the hall, just in the place where idol worshipers would erect an altar to their gods It was in imitation of a tumulus destined to receive some relic of the revered teacher, and the genius of the architect had artfully designed the construction of the cave so that the rays of the sun fell upon the dagoba and surrounded its mysterious presence with a halo of light.

The monks intoned a solemn chant, and its long-drawn cadences filled the hall with a spirit of sanctity, impressing the hearers as though Buddha himself had descended on its notes from his blissful rest in Nirvâna to instruct, to convert, and to gladden his faithful disciples.

The monks chanted a hymn, of which the novice could catch some of the lines as they were sung; and these were the words that rang in his ears:

> "In the mountain hall we are taking our seats,
> In solitude calming the mind;
> Still are our souls, and in silence prepared
> By degrees the truth to find."

When they had circumambulated the dagoba, they halted in front of it where the novice now discovered an image of the Buddha in the attitude of teaching, and the monks spoke in chorus:

"I am anxious to lead a life of purity to the end of my earthly career when my life will return to the precious trinity of the Buddha, the Truth and the Brotherhood."

Then the chanting began again:

> "Vast as the sea
> Our heart shall be,
> And full of compassion and love.
> Our thoughts shall soar

Forevermore
High. like the mountain dove.

"We anxiously yearn
From the Master to learn,
Who found the path of salvation.
We follow His lead
Who taught us to read
The problem of origination.[8]"

A venerable old monk who performed the duties of abbot now stepped forth and asked the assembled brethren whether any one had a communication to make that deserved the attention of the assemblage, and after the question had been repeated three times Subhûti, one of the older monks, said:

"There is a young man with us who, having left the world, stayed with me some time for the sake of instruction and discipline. He is here and desires to be admitted to the brotherhood."

The abbot replied: "Let him come forward."

It was Charaka; and when he stepped into the midst of the brethren, the abbot viewed his tall figure with a kindly, searching glance and asked: "What is your name and what your desire?"

Charaka knelt down and said with clasped hands: "My name is Charaka. I entreat the Brotherhood for initiation. May the Brotherhood receive me and raise me up to their height of spiritual perfection. Have compassion on me, reverend sirs, and grant my request."

The abbot then asked the supplicant a series of questions as prescribed in the regulations of the brotherhood: whether he was free from contagious disease, whether he was a human being, a man, and of age, whether his own master and not a slave nor in the king's service; whether unencumbered with debts and whose disciple he was.

When all the questions had been answered satisfactorily, the abbot submitted the case to the brotherhood, saying: "Reverend sirs, the Brotherhood may hear me. This man Charaka, a disciple of the venerable Subhûti, desires to receive the ordination. He is free from all obstacles to ordination. He has an alms-bowl and a yellow robe, and entreats the

Brotherhood for ordination, with the reverent brother Subhûti as his teacher. Let those among the venerable brethren who are in favor of granting the ordination be silent. Let those who are opposed to it step forth and speak."

These words were three times repeated, and as there was no dissenting voice, the abbot declared with solemnity: "The Brotherhood indicates by its silence that it grants to Charaka the ordination, with the reverend brother Subhûti as his teacher."

Having completed the ceremony and having recited the rules of the order including the four great prohibitions, viz., that an ordained monk must abstain from carnal indulgence, from theft of any kind, from killing even the meanest creature, and from boasts of miraculous powers, the abbot requested the novice to pronounce the refuge formula, which Charaka repeated three times in a clear and ringing voice. Then the congregation again intoned a chant, and, having circumambulated the dagoba, left the assembly hall, marching in solemn procession along the aisles, each brother thereupon betaking himself to his cell.

THE NOVICE.

CHARAKA the novice lived with his brethren in peace, and his senior, the venerable Subhûti, was proud of his learned disciple, for he was patient, docile, modest, earnest, and intelligent, and proved all these good qualities by an abnormally rapid progress. He learned the Sutras perfectly and soon knew them better than his teacher. He had a sonorous voice, and it was a pleasure to hear him recite the sacred formulas or chant the verses proclaiming the glorious doctrine of the Blessed One. To all appearances the Brotherhood had made a good acquisition; but if the venerable Subhûti could have looked into the heart of Charaka he would have beheld a different state of things, for the soul of the novice was full of impatience, dissatisfaction, and excitement. The life of a monk was so different from what he had expected and his dearest hopes found no fulfilment.

Charaka had learned many beautiful sentiments from the mouth of his teacher; some of them fascinated him by the melodious intonation of their rhythm, some by the philosophical depth of their meaning, some by their truth and lofty morality. How delighted was he with the lines:

> "Earnestness leads to the State Immortal;
> Thoughtlessness is dreary Yama's portal.
> Those who earnest are will never die,
> While the thoughtless in death's clutches lie."[4]

How powerfully was he affected by the following stanza:

> "With goodness meet an evil deed,
> With lovingkindness conquer wrath,
> With generosity quench greed,
> And lies, by walking in truth's path."[5]

But sometimes he was startled and had difficulty in understanding the sense. He wanted peace, not tranquilisation; he wanted Nirvâna, its bliss, and its fulness, not extinction. And yet sometimes it seemed as if the absolute obliteration of his activity were expected of him:

"Only if like a broken gong
Thou utterest no sound:
Then hast thou reached Nirvana,
And the end of strife hast found."[6]

Yet Charaka said to himself: "It is only the boisterous noise that must be suppressed, not work; only evil intention, not life itself; the weeds, not the wheat." For it is said:

"What should be done, ye do it,
Nor let pass by the day:
With vigor do your duty,
And do it while you may."[7]

Not life, but error and vice, must be attacked. Not existence is evil, but vanity, anger, and sloth:

"As fields are damaged by a bane,
So 'tis conceit destroys the vain.
As palaces are burned by fire,
The angry perish in their ire.
And as strong iron is gnawed by rust,
So fools are wrecked through sloth and lust."[8]

What ambition was beaming in the eyes of Charaka! The venerable Subhûti thought, there is but one danger for this noble novice: it is this, that the brethren may discover his brightness and spoil him by flattery. Instead of freeing himself from the fetters of the world, he may be entangled in the meshes of a spiritual vanity, which, being more subtle, is more perilous than the lust of the world and of its possessions. Then he recited to Charaka the lines:

"No path anywhere
Leadeth through the air.
The multitude delights
In sacrificial rites.
Throughout the world
Ambition is unfurled;
But from all vanity
Tathagatas are free."[9]

Charaka knew that there were fools among men considered saints, who claimed to walk through the air. He was not credulous, but when told that to attempt the performance of supernatural deeds was vanity, his ambition revolted against the idea of setting limits to human invention. Man might find paths through the air as well as over water; and he submitted to the sentiment only because he regarded it as a form of discipline by which he would learn to rise higher. So he suppressed his ambition, thinking that if he only abode his time he would find himself richly rewarded by the acquisition of spiritual powers which would be a blessing forever, an imperishable treasure that could not be lost by the accidents of life and would not share the doom of compounds which in due time must be dissolved again. He was yearning for life, not for death, for a fulness of melody and a wealth of harmony, not for the stillness of the broken gong. He had seen the world and he knew life in all its phases. He disdained loud noise and coarse enjoyments but he had not left his home and wandered into homelessness to find the silence of the tomb. A chill came over him, and he shrank from the ideal of sainthood as though it were the path to mental suicide. "No, no!" he groaned, "I am not made to be a monk. Either I am too sinful for a holy life, or the holiness of the cloister is not the path of salvation."

THE GOD PROBLEM.

BUDDHISM had gained ascendency in India without exterminating the more ancient creeds, and there were many devoutly religious people who had only a vague notion of the contrast in which it stood to other forms of faith.

The spiritual atmosphere in which Charaka had grown up consisted of a mixture of all the thoughts, influences, and opinions then entertained in India; but while the northern gods that had been worshiped by the ancestors of the invaders in their former homes had faded from the mental vision of the present generation, the ancient deities of India had not gained full recognition. Vishnu, Shiva, and Indra appeared to them as the patrons of conquered races and were therefore deemed of inferior power. Among the better educated Hindu people philosophical ideas were spreading and

Brahma was revered as the Supreme Being, the Great, the Omnipotent, the Omnipresent, as the All-Consciousness and All-Perfection, the Creator, the Fashioner, the Ruler of the Universe, and the All-Father of all beings. With this God-idea of an all-embracing personal deity Charaka had become familiar almost from childhood and he was greatly astonished not to hear a word about God, the Lord, or Brahma, in his religious instructions.

Buddha was spoken of as the teacher of gods and men; he was worshiped with a reverence which was peculiar to him; but the belief in the ancient gods was not disturbed. Their existence was neither denied nor affirmed.

So long as he was unacquainted with his new surroundings, Charaka did not dare to ask questions, but when he began to know his kind-hearted elder Subhûti and some others of the monks, he grew more assured, and one day while several brothers were seated at the portico of the assembly hall, he ventured to inquire as to the doctrine concerning God.

Life is taken seriously in a Buddhist monastery and the tone of conversation is always religious and considerate. Nevertheless there were never missing among the brethren men of a lighter temper, who saw the humor of things, who could smile and, smiling, point out the comical features of life so as to make their fellow brethren smile too, for real laughter was seldom, or never, heard in the precincts of the cloister. We find frequent traces of this humor in the wall paintings as well as the legends of saints, part of which are preserved even to-day. Now when Charaka spoke of God, one of the brethren, Kevaddha by name, a healthy looking man of medium size and of radiant face, drew near and asked, "What do you mean,—Indra, the thunderer, the soma-intoxicated braggart-hero and ruler of the second heaven, whom the people call Sakra or Vâsava—or do you mean Shiva, the powerful and terrible One, decked with a necklace of skulls, the god full of awe and majesty? Perhaps you mean Vishnu, in any of his avatars, as a fish or a wild boar or a white horse?"

Charaka shook his head, and Kevaddha continued: "May be you mean Krishna, the avatar of love, he who danced with all the shepherdesses at once, finding an appropriate incarnation in their favorite swains, while each girl imagined that she alone held the god in her arms?"

"My question refers to no one of the gods," replied the novice, "but to God," and the emphasis with which he marked the difference showed that he felt not like joking on a problem which was of grave importance to him.

"Ah, I see!" exclaimed Kevaddha. His lip curled with sarcasm and there was a twinkle of triumph in his eye, for the topic under discussion reminded him of a contest which he had had with a Brahman priest in which his antagonist had been completely worsted by his superior skill in pointing out the weak side of the proposition and holding it up to ridicule. "Ah, I see!" he exclaimed, "you do not mean any one of the several gods, but god in general. You are like the man who sent his servant to market to buy fruit and when the latter returned with bananas, mangoes, grapes, and an assortment of other fruit, he upbraided him, saying: 'I do not want bananas, nor mangoes, nor grapes, nor pears, nor prunes, nor apples, nor pomegranates, I want fruit! Fruit I want —fruit pure and undefiled, not a particular fruit, but fruit in general!' "

Said Charaka: "Are you a wrangler, famous in the art of dialectics and you know not the difference between God and the gods? I love God but I hate the gods!"

"Is it possible," cried Kevaddha with a sarcastic chuckle, "you hate the gods and you love God? Can you hate all the single men, monks and laymen, traders, warriors, kings, noblemen, Brahmans, Kshatryas, and Shudras, and love man in general? How is it that you can hate the gods and love God? Does not the general include the particular?"

"Be so good, reverend sir," answered the novice, who began to chafe under the attacks of the brisk monk, "to understand what I mean. The world in which we live is a world of order, and we know that there are laws to which we must submit. When I speak of God I mean him who made us, the Omnipotent Creator of the Universe, the Father of all Beings, the Standard of all Perfection, the Eternal Law of Life."

"Well, well," replied Kevaddha, who though boisterous was at the bottom of his heart good-natured. "I do not mean to offend. I try to drive a truth home to you in the guise of fun. The truth is serious, though my mode of expression may be humorous. I understand now that you are devoted to the great All-God, Brahma, as the Brahmans call him, the Lord, Creator and Ruler of the Universe. But did you ever consider two things, first that such an All-God conceived as a being that has name and form is the product of our own imagination as much as are all other deities of the people; and secondly, if Brahma were as real as you are and I am, he would be of no avail? Every one must find the path of salvation himself, and Brahma's wisdom is not your wisdom. Nor can Brahma who resides in the Brahma heaven teach you anything."

Charaka did not conceal his dissatisfaction with Kevaddha's notion of God and said: "The mere idea that there is a God gives me strength. He may be directly unapproachable or may surround us as the air or as the ether which penetrates our bodies. He may be different from what we surmise him to be; but he must exist as the cause of all that is good, and wise, and true, and beautiful. How shall I, in my endeavors to seek the truth, succeed if there be no eternal standard of truth?"

"Yes, I know," replied Kevaddha with undisguised condescension; "It will help a youth who pursues an ideal to think of it as a being, as a god, as the great god, as the greatest god of all. Children need toys and the immature need gods. Your case reminds me of a story which was told me when I in my younger years went out not unlike you in search of truth."

"Tell us the story!" exclaimed one of the younger brethren, and Kevaddha said: "If I were sure not to hurt the feelings of our young friend, the novice, I should be glad to tell the story. But seeing that he is a worshiper of Brahma, I had better let the matter drop!"

Charaka answered: "I am not a worshiper of Brahma, unless you understand by Brahma the First Cause of the All, the ultimate reason of existence, the Supreme Being, the Perceiver of all things, the Controller, the Lord, the Maker, the Fashioner, the Chief, the Victor, the Ruler, the Father of all beings who ever have been and are to be! If your story be instructive I am anxious to hear it myself, even though it should criticise my belief."

All further discussion ceased when Kevaddha showed his readiness to tell the story.

KEVADDHA'S STORY.

"THERE was a priest in Benares, a man of Brahman caste, learned in all the wisdom of the Vedas, not of the common type of priests but an honest searcher after truth. He longed for peace of heart and was anxious to reach Nirvâna; yet he could not understand how it was possible in the flesh to attain perfect tranquillity, for life is restless and in none of the four states of aggregation can that calmness be found which is the condition of the blissful state. So, this priest thought to himself: 'Before I can make any progress, I must solve the question, Where do the four states of aggregation: the solid state, the watery state, the fiery state, and the state of air, utterly cease?'

"Having prepared his mind, the priest entered into a trance in which the path to the gods became revealed to him, and he drew near to where the four great kings of the gods were. And having drawn near, he addressed the four great kings as follows: 'My friends, where do the four states of aggregation: the solid state, the watery state, the fiery state, and the state of air, utterly cease?' When he had thus spoken, the four great kings answered and said: 'We gods, O priest, do not know where the four states of aggregation utterly cease. However, O priest, there are the gods of the higher heavens, who are more glorious and more excellent than we. They would know where the four states of aggregation utterly cease.'

"When the four great kings had thus spoken the priest visited the gods of the higher heavens and approached their ruler, Ishvara. He propounded the same question and received the same answer. Ishvara, the Lord, advised the priest to go to Yâma. 'He is powerful and has charge over the souls of the dead. He is apt to be versed in problems that are profound and recondite and abstruse and occult. Go to Yâma; he may know where the four states of aggregation utterly cease.'

"The priest acted upon Ishvara's advice, and went to Yâma, but the result was the same. Yâma sent the priest to the satisfied gods, whose chief ruler is the Great Satisfied One. 'They are the gods who are pleased with whatever is. They are the gods of serenity and contentment. If there is any one who can answer your question, they will be able to tell you where the four states of aggregation utterly cease.'

"The priest went to the heaven of the satisfied gods, but here too he was disappointed. Their ruler, the Great Satisfied One, said: 'I, O priest, do not know where these four states of aggregation, the solid state, the watery state, the fiery state, and the state of air, utterly cease. However, O priest, there are the gods of the retinue of Brahma, who are more glorious and more excellent than I. They would know where these four states of aggregation utterly cease.'

"Then, this same priest entered again upon a state of trance, in which his thoughts found the way to the Brahma world. There the priest drew near to where the gods of the retinue of Brahma were, and having drawn near, he spake to the gods of the retinue of Brahma as follows: 'My friends, where do these four states of aggregation, the solid state, the watery state, the fiery state, and the state of air, utterly cease?'

"When he had thus spoken, the gods of the retinue of Brahma answering spake as follows: 'We, O priest, cannot answer your question. However, there is Brahma, the great Brahma, the First Cause of the All, the Supreme Being, the All-Perfection, the All-Perceiving One, theController, the Lord of All, the Creator, the Fashioner, the Chief, the Victor, the Ruler, the All-Father, he who is more glorious, more excellent, than all celestial beings, he will know where the four states of aggregation, the solid state, the watery state, the fiery state, and the state of air, do utterly cease.'

"Said the priest: 'But where, my friends, is the great Brahma at the present moment?' And the gods answered: 'We do not know, O priest, where the great Brahma is, or in what direction the great Brahma can be found. But inasmuch, O priest, as he is omnipresent, you will see signs and notice a radiance and the appearance of an effulgence, and then Brahma will appear. This is the previous sign of the appearance of Brahma, that a radiance is noticed, or an effulgence appears.'

"The priest, having invoked Brahma's appearance with due reverence and according to the rules of the Vedas, in a short time Brahma appeared. Then the priest drew near to where Brahma was, and having drawn near, he spake to Brahma as follows: 'My friend, where do the four states of aggregation, the solid state, the watery state, the fiery state, and the state of air, utterly cease?'

"When he had thus spoken, the great Brahma opened his mouth and spake as follows: 'I, O priest, am Brahma, the great Brahma, the Supreme Being, the All-Perfection, the All-Perceiving One, the Controller, the Lord of All, the Creator, the Fashioner, the Chief, the Victor, the Ruler, the All-Father.'

"A second time the priest asked his question, and the great Brahma gave him the same answer, saying: 'I, O priest, am Brahma, the great Brahma, the Supreme Being, the All-Perfection;' and he did not cease until he had enumerated all the titles applied to him.

"Having patiently listened to Brahma, the priest repeated his question a third time, and added: 'I am not asking you, my friend, Are you Brahma, the great Brahma, the Supreme Being, the All-Perfection, the All-Perceiver, the All-Father, and whatever titles and accomplishments you may have in addition; but this, my friend, is what I ask you: 'Where do the four states of aggregation, the solid state, the watery state, the fiery state, and the state or air, utterly cease?'

"The great Brahma remained unmoved, and answered a third time, saying: 'I, O priest, am Brahma, the great Brahma, the Supreme Being, the All-Perfection, the All-Perceiver,' enumerating again all the titles applied to him.

"Now the priest rose and said: 'Are you truly a living being, or an automaton, that you can do nothing but repeat a string of words?'

"And now the great Brahma rose from his seat and approached the priest, and leading him aside to a place where he could not be overheard by any of the gods, spake to him as follows: 'The gods of my suite and all the worshipers of the world that honor me with sacrifice and adoration, believe that Brahma sees all things, knows all things, has penetrated all things; therefore, O priest, I answered you as I did in the presence of the gods. But I will tell you, O priest, in confidence, that I do not know where the four states of aggregation, the solid state, the watery state, the fiery state, and the state of air, utterly cease. It was a mistake, O priest, that you left the earth where the Blessed One resides, and came up to heaven in quest of an answer which cannot be given you here. Turn back, O priest, and having drawn near to the Blessed One, the Enlightened Buddha, ask him your question, and as the Blessed One shall explain it to you, so believe.'

"Thereupon the priest, as quickly as a strong man might stretch out his bent arm, disappeared from the Brahma heaven and appeared before the Blessed One; and he greeted the Blessed One and sat down respectfully at one side, and spake to the Blessed One as follows: 'Reverend Sir, where do the four states of aggregation, the solid state, the watery state, the fiery state, and the state of air, utterly cease?'

"When he had thus spoken the Blessed One answered as follows: 'Once upon a time, O priest, some sea-faring traders had a land-sighting bird when they sailed out into the sea; and when the ship was in mid-ocean they set free that land-sighting bird. This bird flies in an easterly direction, in a southerly direction, in a westerly direction, and in a northerly direction, and to the intermediate quarters, and if it sees land anywhere it flies thither, but if it does not see land it returns to the the ship. In exactly the same way, O priest, when you had searched as far as the Brahma world and found no answer to your question you returned to the place whence you came. The question, O priest, ought never to have been put thus: Where do these four states of aggregation cease? The question ought to be as follows:

"Oh! Where can water, where can wind,
Where fire and earth no footing find?

Where disappear all mine and thine,
Good, bad, long, short, and coarse and fine,
And where do name and form both cease
To find in nothingness release?"

" 'The answer, however, is this:

"'Tis in the realm of radiance bright,
Invisible, eternal light,
And infinite, a state of mind,
There water, earth, and fire, and wind,
And elements of any kind,
Will nevermore a footing find;
There disappear all mine and thine,
Good, bad, long, short, and coarse, and fine,
There too will name and form both cease,
To find in nothingness release."

"Then the priest understood that the world of matter is restless and remains restless, but peace of heart is a condition of mind which must be acquired by self-discipline, by wisdom, by devotion. The gods cannot help; nor even can Brahma himself, the Great Brahma, the Supreme Being, the Lord and Creator. Sacrifice is useless and prayer and worship are of no avail. But if we desire to attain the highest state of bliss, which is Nirvâna, we must follow the Blessed One, the Teacher of gods and men; and like him we must by our own effort become lamps unto ourselves and resolutely walk upon the noble eightfold path."[10]

THE CONFESSION.

THE young novice spent his days in study and his nights in doubt. He followed with interest the recitations of his instructor on the philosophy of the Enlightened One; he enjoyed the birthstories of Bodhisattva and the parables of the master with their moral applications, but when he retired in the evening or was otherwise left to his own thoughts he began to ponder on the uselessness of the hermit's life and longed to return to the world with its temptations and struggles, its victories and defeats, its pleasures and pains, its hopes and fears. He enjoyed the solitude of the forest, but he began to think that the restlessness of the world could offer him more peace of mind than the inactivity of a monkish life.

When Charaka had familiarised himself with all the Sutras and wise sayings which were known to the brethren of the monastery, the time began to hang heavy on his hands, and he felt that the religious discourses were becoming tedious.

Weeks elapsed, and Charaka despaired of either becoming accustomed to monkish life or of understanding the deeper meaning of their renunciation of the world, and his conscience began to trouble him; for the more the elder brethren respected him for his knowledge and gentleness, and the more they praised him, the less worthy he deemed himself of their recognition.

The day of confession approached again. He had spent the hours in fasting and self-discipline, but all this availed nothing. He was weary and felt a sadness of heart beyond description.

In the evening all the brethren were gathered together in the chaitya, the large hall where they held their devotional meetings. The aisles lay in mystic darkness, and the pictures on the heavy columns and on the ceiling were half concealed. They appeared and disappeared from time to time in the flicker of the torches that were employed to light the room.

The monks sat in silent expectation, their faces showing a quietude and calmness which proved that they were unconcerned about their own fate, ready to live or to die, as their doom might be, only bent on the aim of reaching Nirvâna.

The senior monk arose and addressed the assembly. "Reverend sirs," he said, "let the order hear me. To-day is full moon, and the day of the unburdening of our hearts. If the order is ready, let the order consecrate this day to the recital of the confession. This is our first duty, and so let us listen to the declaration of purity."

The brethren responded, saying: "We are here to listen and will consider the questions punctiliously."

The speaker continued: "Whoever has committed a transgression, let him speak, those who are free from the consciousness of guilt, let them be silent."

At this moment a tall figure rose slowly and hesitatingly from the ground at the further end of the hall. He did not speak but stood there quietly, towering for some time in the dusky recess between two pillars as though he were the apparition of a guilty conscience. The presiding brother at last broke the silence and addressed the brethren, saying: "A monk who has committed a fault, and remembers it, if he endeavors to be pure, should confess his fault. When a fault is confessed it will lie lightly upon him."

Still the shadowy figure stood motionless, which seemed to increase the gloom in the hall.

"One of the brethren has risen, indicating thereby that he desires to speak," continued the abbot. "A monk who does not confess a fault after the question has been put three times is guilty of an intentional lie, and the Blessed One teaches that an intentional lie cuts a man off from sanctification."

The gloomy figure now lifted his head and with suppressed emotion began to speak. "Venerable father," he said, "and ye, reverend sirs, may I speak out and unburden my heart?" The voice was that of the novice, and a slight commotion passed through the assemblage. Having been encouraged to speak freely and without reserve, Charaka began:

"Venerable father, and ye, reverend sirs: I feel guilty of having infringed on one of the great prohibitions. I am as a palm tree, the top of which has been destroyed. I am broken in spirit and full of contrition. I am anxious to be a disciple of the Shakya-Muni, but I am not worthy to be a monk, I never have been and I never shall be." Here his voice faltered, and he sobbed like a child.

The brethren were horror-stricken; they thought at once that the youth was contaminated by some secret crime; he was too young to be free from passion, too beautiful to be beyond temptation, too quick-witted not to be ambitious. True, they loved him, but they felt now that their affection for him was a danger, and there was no one in the assembly who did not feel the youth's self-accusation as partly directed against himself. But the abbot overcame the sentiment that arose so quickly, and encouraged the penitent brother to make a full confession. "Do not despair," he said, "thou art young; it is natural that thy heart should still cherish dreams of love, and that alluring reminiscences should still haunt thy mind."

"I entered the brotherhood with false hopes and wrong aspirations," replied the novice. "I am longing for wisdom and supernatural powers; I am ambitious to do and to dare, and I hoped to acquire a deeper knowledge through self-discipline and holiness. I am free from any actual transgression, but my holiness is mockery; my piety is not genuine; I am a hypocrite and I find that I am belying you, venerable father, and all the monks of this venerable community. But it grieveth me most that I am false to myself; I am not worthy to wear the yellow robe."

"Thou art not expected to be perfect," replied the abbot, "thou art walking on the path, and hast not as yet reached the goal. Thy fault is impatience with thyself and not hypocrisy."

"Do not palliate my fault, venerable father," said Charaka. "There is something wrong in my heart and in my mind. If I am not a hypocrite, then I am a heretic; and a heretic walks on the wrong road in the wrong direction, and can never reach the goal. Do not extenuate, do not qualify and mitigate my faults, for I feel their grievousness and am anxious to be led out of the darkness into the light. I long for life and the unfoldment of life. I want to comprehend the deepest truths; I want to know and to taste the highest bliss; I want to accomplish the greatest deeds."

"Then thou art worldly; thou longest for power, for fame, for honor, for pleasures," suggested the abbot inquiringly; "thou art not yet free from the illusion of selfhood. It is not the truth, then, that thou wantest, but thyself, to be an owner of the truth; it is self-enhancement, not service; vanity, not helpfulness."

"That may be, reverend father," replied the novice; "thy wisdom shall judge me; though I do not feel myself burdened by selfishness. No, I do not love myself. I would gladly sacrifice myself for any noble cause, for truth, for justice, for procuring bliss for others. Nor do I crave for worldly pleasures, but I do not feel any need of shirking them. Pleasures like pains are the stuff that life is made of, and I do not hate life. I enjoy the unfoldment of life with all its aspirations, not for my sake, but for life's sake. I do not love myself, I love God. That is my fault, and that is the root from which grow all my errors, heresies, hypocrisies, and the false position in which I now am."

The good abbot did not know what to say. He looked at the poor novice and pitied him for his pangs of conscience. Every one present felt that the man suffered, that there was something wrong with him; but no one could exactly say what it was. His ambition was not sinful but noble. And that he loved God was certainly not a crime. At last the abbot addressed Subhûti, Charaka's senior and teacher, and asked him: "Have you, reverend brother, noticed in this novice's behavior or views anything strange or exceptional?"

Subhûti replied that he had not.

The abbot continued to inquire about Charaka's previous religious relations and the significance of his love of God.

"I do not know, reverend sir," was the elder monk's answer. "He is not a Brahman, but a descendant of a noble family of the northern conquerors that came to India and founded the kingdom of Gandhâra. Yet he knows Brahman writings and is familiar with the philosophy of the Yavanas[12] of the distant West. I discoursed with him and understand that by God he means all that is right and good and true in the world and without whom there can be no enlightenment."

"Very well," proclaimed the abbot, "there is no sin in loving God, for what you describe as God is our Lord Shakyamuni, the Enlightened One, the Buddha, the Tathâgata;" but he added not without a suggestion of reproof: "You might dignify the Lord Buddha with a higher title than God. Gods, if they exist, are not Buddha's equals. When Bodhisattva was a child, the gods prostrated themselves before him, for they recognised the Tathâgata's superiority even before he had attained to complete Buddhahood. The divinity of the gods is less than the noble life of a Bodhisattva."

Having thus discussed the case of the novice Charaka, the abbot addressed himself to the Brotherhood, asking the reverend sirs what they would deem right in the present case. Was the brother at all guilty of the fault of which he accused himself and if so what should he do to restore his good standing and set himself aright in the Brotherhood?

Then Subhûti arose and said: "Charaka is a man of deep comprehension and of an earnest temper. The difficulty which he encounters is not for us to judge him or to advise him about. But there is a philosopher living in the kingdom of Magadha, by the name of Açvaghosha. If there is any one in the world that can set an erring brother right, it is Açvoghosha, whose wisdom is so great that since Buddha entered Nirvâna there has been no man on earth who might have surpassed him either in knowledge or judgment." So Subhûti proposed to write a letter of introduction to Açvaghosha commending the brother Charaka to his care and suggesting to him to dispel his doubts and to establish him again firmly in the faith in which the truth shines forth more brilliantly than in any other religion.

The abbot agreed with Subhûti and the general opinion among the brethren was in favor of sending Charaka to the kingdom of Magadha to the philosopher Açvaghosha to have his doubts dispelled and his heart established again in the faith of Buddha, the Blessed One, the teacher of truth.

Before they could carry out their plan the session was interrupted by a messenger from the royal court of Gandhâra, who inquired for a novice by the name of Charaka,—a man well versed in medicine and other learned arts. A dreadful epidemic had spread in the country, and the old king had died while two of his sons were afflicted with the disease and now lay at the point of death. The oldest son and heir to the throne was in the field defending his country against the Parthians, and some mountaineers of the East, nominally subject to the kingdom of Magadha but practically independent had utilised the opportunity afforded by these circumstances to descend into the fertile valleys of Gandhâra and to pillage the country.

The regard in which Charaka had been held in the Brotherhood during his novitiate had not suffered through his confession and was even heightened. It had been known in the cloister that the young novice was of a noble family, but he had made nothing of it and so the intimate connection with the royal family of the country created an uncommon sensation among his venerable brethren. Now, a special awe attached to his person since it was known that the young king knew of Charaka, and needing his wisdom, sent a special messenger to call him back to the capital.

In spite of the interruption the ceremony of confession was continued and closed in the traditional way; all the questions regarding transgressions that might have been committed were asked and in some cases sins were punctiliously reported by those who felt a need of unburdening their conscience. Penances were imposed which were willingly and submissively assumed. When everything had been attended to, the abbot turned again to Charaka saying, "If you had concealed your secret longings, you would have been guilty of hypocrisy, but now since you have openly laid bare the state of your mind, there is no longer any falsehood in you. Therefore I find no fault with your conduct; should you find that you cannot remain a monk, you must know that there is no law that obliges you to remain in the Brotherhood against your will."

The abbot then granted Charaka permission to obey the King's call, saying, "You are free to leave the order in peace and goodwill, but I enjoin you to make a vow that you will not leave your doubts unsettled, but that as soon as you have attended to the pressing duties which will engage your attention at the capital you will make a pilgrimage to the philosopher Açvaghosha, who lives in the kingdom of Magadha. He will be a better adviser than I, and he shall decide whether or not you are fit to be a monk of our Lord the Buddha."

GANDHARA.

AS the night was far advanced, the royal messenger allowed his horses a short rest in the Vihâra, and set out with Charaka at an early hour the following morning. The two travelers could not, however, make rapid progress, for the atmosphere was murky, and the fogs of the rainy season obscured the way. They passed a picket of Gandhâra soldiers who were on the lookout for the hostile mountaineers. The mounted messenger showed them his passport, and the two men reached the capital only when the shades of evening were settling upon the valley. The gates were carefully guarded by armed men. The sentinel led the two horsemen to the officer at the gate, who seemed satisfied with the report that Charaka had nowhere encountered enemies; but the home news was very bad, for one of the princes had died and Chandana (commonly called Kanishka), the third and youngest son of the king, was thought to be critically ill.

The night was darker than usual, and the town made a gloomy impression. The inhabitants were restless and seemed to be prepared for a dire calamity.

Charaka was at once conducted to the royal palace. He passed through a line of long streets which seemed narrow and dismal. The people whom they met on their way, being wrapped in a veil of mist, resembled even at a short distance dim dusky specters, like guilty ghosts condemned for some crime to haunt the scene of their former lives. At last they reached the palace, and Charaka was ushered into the dimly lighted bedroom of Prince Kanishka. Charaka stood motionless and watched the heavy breathing of the patient. He then put his hand gently upon the feverish forehead and in a low voice demanded water to cool the burning temples of the sick man. Turning to the attendants, he met the questioning eye of a tall and beautiful woman, an almost imperious figure. He knew her well; it was Princess Kamalavatî, the king's daughter and a younger half-sister of the prince.

"His condition is very bad," whispered Charaka in reply to the unuttered question that was written in her face, "but not yet hopeless. Where are the nurses who assist you in ministering unto the patient?"

Two female attendants appeared, and the physician withdrew with them into an adjoining room where he listened to their reports. "The king and his second son have died of the same disease, and the situation is very critical," said Charaka; "but we may avoid the mistakes made in the former cases and adjust the diet strictly to the condition of the patient."

Charaka and Kanishka were of the same age. They had for some time been educated together and were intimate friends. But when the prince joined the royal army, Charaka studied the sciences under the direction of Jîvaka, the late court physician of Gandhâra, and knowing how highly the latter had praised the young man as his best disciple, the prince had unbounded confidence in the medical skill of his boyhood companion. He had suggested calling him when his father, the king, fell sick, but his advice had remained unheeded, and now being himself ill, he was impatient to have the benefit of his friend's assistance.

Charaka gave his instructions to the princess and the other attendants and then sat down quietly by the bedside of the patient. When Kanishka awoke from his restless slumber, he extended his hand and tried to speak, but the physician hushed him, saying: "Keep quiet, and your life will be saved."

"I will be quiet," whispered Kanishka, not without great effort, "but save my life,—for the sake of my country, not for my own sake." After a pause he continued: "Tell my sister to call Matura, our brave and faithful Matura, to my bedside."

Matura, the scion of a noble Gandhâra family, had served his country on several occasions and was at present at the capital. He came and waited patiently till Charaka gave him permission to see the patient.

In this interview the prince explained to Matura the political situation since his father's death. His royal brother, now in the field against the Parthians, was at present the legitimate king. "During his absence," said Kanishka, "the duty devolves on me, as the vicegerent of the crown, to keep the mountaineers out of the kingdom, and I call upon you to serve me as a chancellor in this critical situation. Raise troops to expel the marauders, but at the same time exhaust diplomatic methods by appealing to the honor and dignity of the kingdom of Magadha of which these robber tribes are nominal subjects."

Thus Matura took charge of state affairs and Charaka and Kamalavatî united in attending to the treatment of the sick prince. They had weary nights and hours of deep despondency when they despaired of the recovery of their beloved patient, but the crisis came and Kanishka survived it. He regained strength, first slowly, very slowly, then more rapidly, until he felt that he was past all danger.

The rainy season had given the people of Gandhâra a respite from the suffering caused by the hostilities of their enemies. The king, Kanishka's elder brother, continued to wage war against the Parthians and concentrated his forces for striking a decisive blow. But while the best troops of the country had thus still to be employed against a formidable foe, the mountaineers renewed their raids, and the king of Magadha, too weak to interfere with his stubborn vassals, pleaded their cause declaring that they had grievances against the kingdom of Gandhâra and could therefore not be restrained. The prince accordingly declared war on the kingdom of Magadha. He raised an army, and the young men of the peasantry, who had suffered much from this state of unrest, gladly allowed themselves to be enlisted.

KING KANISHKA.

DURING the preparations for war against Magadha there came tidings from the Parthian frontier that the troops of Gandhâra had gained a decisive victory which, however, was dearly bought, for the king himself who had been foremost among the combatants, died a glorious death on the field of battle. The crown now passed to Kanishka who deemed it his first duty to overcome the enemies of his nation. Leaving the trusted generals of his brother in command of the victorious army in Parthia, he placed himself at the head of the troops destined to march against Magadha. Charaka was requested to accompany him in the field, and Matura remained behind as chancellor of the state.

Charaka loved the princess without knowing it. She had been kindly disposed toward him from childhood; but her interest was heightened to admiration since she had observed him at the bedside of her brother. How noble he was, how thoughtful, how unselfish; and at the same time how wise in spite of his youth. When the two parted she said: "Take care of my brother, be to him as a guardian angel; and," added the princess smiling, "be good to yourself,—for my sake."

Charaka stood bewildered. He felt his cheeks flushing, and did not know what to think or say. All at once he became conscious of the fact that a powerful yearning had gradually grown up in his heart, and a tender and as yet undefined relation had become established between himself and the princess. He was not sure, however, whether it was right for him to accept and press the beautiful woman's hand that was offered him in unaffected friendliness and with maidenly innocence. He stood before her like a schoolboy censured for a serious breach of the school regulations. He stammered; his head drooped; and at last covering his eyes with his hand, he began to sob like a child with a guilty conscience.

At this moment Kanishka approached to bid

his sister good-by; and after a few words of mutual good wishes Charaka and Kamalavatî parted.

While the king and his physician were riding side by side, their home behind them, their enemy in front, Kanishka inquired about the trouble which had stirred Charaka to tears. And Charaka said: "It is all my fault. When your sister bade me farewell, I became aware of a budding love toward her in my soul, and I feel that she reciprocates my sentiment. I know it is sinful, and I will not yield to temptation, but I am weak, and that brought tears to my eyes. I feel ashamed of myself."

"Do you think love a sin?" inquired the king.

"Is not celibacy the state of holiness," replied Charaka, "and is not marriage a mere concession to worldliness, being instituted for the sake of preventing worse confusion?"

"You ought to know more about it than I," continued Kanishka, "for you devoted yourself to religion by joining the brotherhood, while I am a layman, and my religious notions are not grounded on deeper knowledge."

"Alas!" sighed Charaka, "I am not fit to be a monk. The abbot of the Vihâra could not help me and advised me to have my doubts allayed and the problems of my soul settled by Açvoghosha of Magadha, the great philosopher and saint who is said to understand the doctrine of the Blessed One, the Buddha."

"What is the problem that oppresses you?" inquired King Kanishka. "Is your soul burdened with sin?"

"I am not guilty of a sinful deed, but I feel that my soul is sinful in its aspirations. My heart is full of passion, and I have an ambitious mind. I would perform great deeds, noble and miraculous, and would solve the problem of life; I would fathom the mysteries of being and comprehend the law of existence, its source and its purpose. There is an undefined yearning in my breast, a desire to do and to dare, to be useful to others, to live to the utmost of my faculties, and to be rooted in the mysterious ground from which springs all the life that unfolds itself in the world. I came into being, and I shall pass out of existence. I believe that I existed before I was born, and that I shall exist after my death. But these other incarnations of mine are after all other than myself, other at least than my present existence. I understand very well that I am a reproduction of the life impulses that preceded me, and that I shall continue in subsequent reproductions of my karma. But I feel my present self to be the form of this life which will pass away, and I yearn for a union with that eternal substratum of all life which will never pass away."

Kanishka said: "While I was ill I had occasion to meditate on the problem of life and life's relation to death. Once I was dreaming; and in the dream I was not Prince Kanishka, but a king, not King of Gandhâra, but of some unknown country, and I was leading my men in battle; and it happened, as in the case of my brother, that I was victorious, and the hostile army before me turned in wild flight, but in the moment of victory a dying enemy shot an arrow at me which pierced my heart, and I knew my end was come. There was a pang of death, but it was not an unpleasant sensation, for my last thought was: 'Death in battle is better than to live defeated.'[13] I awoke. A gentle perspiration covered my forehead, and I felt as though I had passed through a crisis in which I had gained a new lease of life. My dream had been so vivid that when I awoke I had the impression that I and all the visions that surrounded me had been annihilated; yet after a while, when my mind was again fully adjusted, the dream appeared empty to me, a mere phantasma and illusion. Will it not be similar, if at the moment of death we make our final entrance into Nirvâna? Nirvâna appears to us in our present existence as a negative state, but our present existence is phenomenal, while Nirvâna is the abiding state."

Charaka replied: "I should think there is much truth in your words. But the Tathâgata teaches that by attaining enlightenment, we shall enter Nirvâna even in this present life; and if we do so, it seems to me that our main advantage lies in the comprehension of the transiency of all bodily existence and the permanence of our spiritual nature. Death has lost its terrors to him who sees the immortal state. He knows that in death he sloughs off the mortal. But here my difficulty begins. I long for Nirvâna only as a means to enrich this present life.

"The Tathâgata teaches that life is suffering, and he is right. I do not doubt it. He has further discovered the way of emancipation, which is the eightfold noble path of righteousness. Now, I love life in spite of its suffering, and I am charmed with love. Love is life-giving, heart-gladdening, courage-inspiring! Oh, I love love, real worldly love! I admire heroism, the wild heroism of the battlefield! I long for wisdom, not the wisdom of the monks, but practical science which teaches us the why and wherefore of things and imparts to us the wizard's power over nature. Now, with all this I love righteousness; I feel the superiority of religious calmness, and the blissfulness of Nirvâna. I do not cling to self, but desire to apply myself: I want a field of activity. All these conflicting thoughts produce in me the longing for a solution: there it lies before me as an ideal which I cannot grasp, and I call it God. Oh, that I could speak to the

Tathâgata face to face; that I could go to him for enlightenment, that I could learn the truth so as to walk on the right path and find peace of soul in the tribulations of life. Since the Lord Buddha is no longer walking with us in the flesh, there is only one man in the world who can help me in my distress, and that is the great disciple of the Blessed Master, the philosopher and saint Açvaghosha of Magadha."

"Açvaghosha of Magadha!" replied the king. "Very well! We are waging war with the king of Magadha. Let the prize of combat be the possession of Açvaghosha!"

MAGADHA.

WAR is always deplorable, but sometimes it cannot be avoided. And if that be the case, far from shunning it, a ruler, responsible for the welfare of his people, should carry it on resolutely and courageously with the one aim in view of bringing it speedily to a happy conclusion.

Such was Kanishka's maxim, and he acted accordingly. Having gathered as strong an army as he could muster, he surprised the mountaineers by coming upon them suddenly with superior forces from both sides. They made a desperate resistance, but he overthrew them and, leaving garrisons in some places of strategic importance, carried the war farther into the heart of the kingdom of Magadha. He descended into the valley of the Ganges, and hurrying by forced marches through the vassal kingdoms of Delhi and Sravasti, the Gandhâra army marched in four columns toward the capital of the country.

Subâhu, king of Magadha, met his adversary in the field near Pâtaliputra with an army that had been rapidly assembled, but he could not stay the invader's victorious progress. In several engagements his troops were scattered to the four winds, his elephants captured, and he was obliged to retire to the fortress of Pâtaliputra. There he was besieged, and when he saw that no hope of escape was left he decided to make no further resistance and sent a messenger to king Kanishka, asking him for terms of peace.

The victor demanded an indemnity of three hundred million gold pieces, a sum which the whole kingdom could not produce.

When the besieged king asked for less severe terms, Kanishka replied: "If you are anxious to procure peace, come out to me in person and I will listen to your proposition. I wish to see you. Let us meet face to face, and we will consider our difficulties."

Subâhu, knowing the uselessness of further resistance, came out with his minister and accompanied by his retinue. He was conducted into the presence of Kanishka, who requested him to be seated.

The king of Magadha complied with the request of his victorious rival with the air of a high-minded man, the guest of his equal. Kanishka frowned upon him. He observed the self-possession of his conquered foe with a feeling of resentment, which, however, was somewhat alloyed with admiration.

After a pause he addressed the royal petitioner as follows: "Why didst thou not render justice to me when I asked for it?"

"My intentions were good," replied Subâhu, "I wanted to preserve peace. The mountaineers are restless, but they are religious and full of faith. Their chieftains assured me the people had only retaliated wrongs that they had suffered themselves. Trying to be fair and just to my vassals, I roused the worse evil of war, and in preserving the peace at home I conjured up the specter of hostility from abroad. He who would avoid trouble sometimes breeds greater misfortune."

"In other words," interrupted King Kanishka sternly, "your weakness prevented you from punishing the evil-doers under your jurisdiction, and being incapable of governing your kingdom, you lost your power and the right to rule."

"Sir," replied the humiliated monarch with calm composure, "thou art the victor and thou canst deal with me at thy pleasure, but if the fortunes of the day had turned against thee, thou mightest stand now before me in the same degraded position in which thou now seest me. But the difference is this: I have a clean conscience; I have proved peaceful; I never gave offence to anybody,—consciously. Thou hast carried the war into my country. Thou art the offender; and shouldst thou condemn me to die, I shall die innocent to be reborn in a happier state under more auspicious conditions. The Lord Buddha be praised!"

Kanishka was astonished at the boldness of the king's speech, but he mastered his anger and replied calmly: "Art thou so ignorant as not to know that a ruler's first duty is justice, and to me justice thou hast refused!"

"Man's first duty is to seek salvation," replied the king of Magadha, "and salvation is not obtained by harshness but by piety."

The king of Gandhâra rose to his feet: "Thou art fitted for a monk, not a monarch. Thou hadst better retire to the cloistered cell of a Vihâra than occupy the throne of a great empire. What is the use of piety if it does not help thee to attend to the duties of thy high office? It leads thee into misery and has cost thee thy throne. The world cannot prosper on the principles which thou followest."

Subâhu seemed imperturbable, and without deigning to look at the incensed face of his vituperator he exclaimed: "What is the world if we but gain salvation? Let all the thrones on earth be lost and whole nations perish if only emancipation can be obtained! We want escape, not secular enhancement."

Kanishka stared at the speaker as if unable to comprehend his frame of mind, and Subâhu without showing any concern quoted a stanza from the Dhammapada, saying:

"The king's mighty chariots of iron will rust,
And also our bodies resolve into dust;

But deeds, 'tis sure,
For aye endure."[14]

Filled with admiration of Subâhu's fortitude, Kanishka said: "I see thou art truly a pious man. But thy piety is not of the right kind. Thy way of escape leads into emptiness, and thy salvation is hollow. This world is the place in which the test of truth must be made; and this life is the time in which it is our duty to attain Nirvâna. But I will not now upbraid thee for thy errors; I will first raise thee to a dignified position in which thou canst answer me and give thy arguments. I understand that thou art a faithful disciple of the Buddha and meanest to do that which is right. I respect thy sincerity and greet thee as a brother. Therefore I will not deprive thee of thy crown and title, but I insist on the penalty of three hundred million gold pieces. Thou shalt remain king with the understanding that henceforth thou takest council with me on all questions of political importance, for I see clearly that thou standest in need of advice. But in place of the three hundred million gold pieces I will accept substitutes which I deem worth that amount. First, thou shalt deliver into my hands the bowl which the Tathâgata, the Blessed Buddha, carried in his hand when he was walking on earth, and, secondly, as a ransom for thy royal person which I hold here besieged in Pâtaliputra I request from thee the philosopher Açvaghosha whose fame has spread through all the countries where the religion of enlightenment is preached."

The vanquished king said: "Truly, the bowl of Buddha and the philosopher Açvaghosha are amply worth three hundred million gold pieces, and yet I must confess that thou art generous and thy conditions of peace are fair."

"Do not call me generous," said Kanishka, embracing the king of Magadha, "I am only worldly wise; and it is not my own wisdom. I have learned the maxims of my politics from the Blessed One, the great Buddha."

ACVAGHOSHA.

BUDDHA'S birthday was celebrated with greater rejoicing than usual in the year following king Kanishka's invasion, which took place in the fifth century after the Nirvâna. The formidable invaders had become friends and the people were joyful that the war clouds had dispersed so rapidly.

Kanishka was in good spirits. He was elated by his success, but it had not made him overbearing, and he was affable to all who approached him. In a short time he had become the most powerful monarch of India, his sway extending far beyond the boundaries of his own kingdom. His generals had been victorious over the Parthians in the far west, and his alliance with the king of Magadha made him practically ruler over the valley of the Ganges. But more effective than his strategy and the might of his armies was the kindness which he showed to his vanquished enemies. Princes of smaller dominions willingly acknowledged his superiority and submitted to him their difficulties because they cherished an unreserved confidence in his fairness and love of justice. Thus was laid the foundation of a great empire upon whose civilisation the religion of the Enlightened One exercised a decided influence. Peace was established, commerce and trade flourished, and Greek sculptors flocked to Gandhâra, transplanting the art of their home to the soil of India.

It was the beginning of India's golden age which lasted as long as the Dharma, the doctrine of the Tathâgata, was kept pure and undefiled. A holy enthusiasm seized the hearts of the people and there were many who felt an anxiety to spread the blessings of religion over the whole world. Missionaries went out who reached Thibet and China and even far-off Japan where they sowed the seeds of truth and spread the blessings of lovingkindness and charity.

Kanishka and the king of Magadha enjoyed each other's company. The two allied monarchs started on a peaceful pilgrimage to the various sacred spots of the country. They visited Lumbinî, the birthplace of the Bodhisattva. Thence passing over the site of Kapilavastu, the residence of Shuddhodana, Buddha's father in the flesh and the haunt of Prince Siddhârtha in his youth, they went to the Bodhi tree at Buddhagaya and returned to the capital Benares, to celebrate the birth festival of the Buddha in the Deer Park, on the very spot where the revered Teacher had set the wheel of truth in motion to roll onward for the best of mankind,—the wheel of truth which no god, no demon, nor any other power, be it human, divine or infernal, should ever be able to turn back.

A procession went out to the holy place and circumambulated the stupa, erected on the sacred spot in commemoration of the memorable event, and the two monarchs, who had but a short time before met as foes on the battlefield, walked together like brothers, preceded by white-robed virgins bearing flowers, and followed by priests chanting gâthâs of the blessings of the good law and swinging censers. No display of arms was made but multitudes of peaceful citizens hailed the two rulers and blessed the magnanimity of the hero of Gandhâra.

When the procession halted, Kanishka and his brother king stood in front of a statue of the Buddha and watched the process of depositing flowers. "Who is the beautiful maiden that is leading the flower carriers?" asked Kanishka of the king of Magadha in a whisper; and the latter replied: "It is Bhadraçrî, my only daughter."

Kanishka followed with his eye the graceful movements of the princess and breathed a prayer: "Adoration to the Buddha!" he said to himself in the silent recesses of his heart. "The Buddha has guided my steps and induced me to make peace before the demons of war could do more mischief. I now vow to myself that if the princess will accept me I shall lead her as queen to my capital and she shall be the mother of the kings of Gandhâra to come. May the Tathâgata's blessing be on us and my people!"

At the stupa of the first sermon of the Buddha, peace was definitely concluded. The king of Magadha delivered to his powerful ally the sacred bowl, a treasure which, though small in size, was esteemed worth more than half the kingdom of Magadha; and Açvaghosha, the old philosopher, was bidden to appear at court and be ready to accompany the ruler of Gandhâra to his home in the northwest of India.

Açvaghosha arrived at the Deer Park in a royal carriage drawn by white horses, and there he was presented to King Kanishka. He bowed reverently and said: "Praised be the Lord Buddha for his blessed teachings! Gladness fills my heart when I think how your majesty treats your vanquished foe. The victorious enemy has become a friend and brother, making an end of all hostility forever."

"Good, my friend," replied Kanishka; "if there is any merit in my action I owe thanks for my karma to the Tathâgata. He is my teacher and I bless the happy day on which I became his disciple. My knowledge, however, is imperfect and even my learned friend Charaka is full of doubts on subjects of grave importance. Therefore I invite you to accompany me to Gandhâra, where my people and myself are sorely in need of your wisdom and experience."

"Your invitation is flattering," said the philosopher, "and it is tendered in kindly words; but I pray you, noble sir, leave me at home. I am an aged man and could scarcely stand the exertion of the journey. But I know a worthy scholar, Jñanayaça, who is well versed in the doctrine of our Lord and much younger than I. He may go in my place; and should I grow stronger I shall be glad to visit you in Gandhâra."

"Charaka!" said the king, "have a room fitted up for Açvaghosha in our residence at Benares, and so long as we remain here he shall pass the time in our company. Let him be present at our meals, and when we rest in the evening from the labors of the day let us listen to the words of the philosopher who is regarded as the best interpreter of the significance of Buddha's teachings."

AMITÂBHA.

ONE evening when King Kanishka together with his friend Charaka enjoyed the company of Açvaghosha, the youthful ruler of Gandhâra turned to the venerable philosopher with this request: "And now, worshipful master, tell us, do we worship in Buddha a god or a man?"

Replied Açvaghosha: "Buddha is neither a god nor a man; he is more than either, for he is perfection incarnate. We worship in Buddha wisdom and goodness, that is, the comprehension and application of the truth, which are the qualities that alone render the gods divine. Truth is eternal, but all actual beings, not even excluding the gods, are transient."

Charaka interposed: "We do not speak of the gods, but of God, which means divinity itself. What would the Buddha have taught about God?"

Kanishka added: "We mean God, not in the sense of Brahma, the principle of existence, nor of Ishvara, a personal Lord and manufacturer of universes, but God as goodness, as truth, as righteousness, as love? Does God in this sense exist or not? Is it a dream or a reality? What is it and how do we know of it?"

"You ask a question to answer which will take a book. But I shall be brief. Certainly, God in this sense is a reality. God, in this sense is the good law that shapes existence, leading life step by step onward and upward toward its highest goal—enlightenment. Recognition of this law gives us light on the conditions of our existence so as to render it possible for us to find the right path; and we call it Dharmakaya, the body of the good law, or Amitâbha, the source of infinite light, or by some other name. It is the norm of all nature involving the bliss of goodness and the curse of wrong doing according to irrefragable causation."

"Accordingly, a man is not a Buddha by birth, but he can become a Buddha by attaining to Buddhahood," said the king inquiringly.

"Exactly so," replied Açvaghosha. "The highest truth is not a fabrication of the mind; the highest truth is eternal.[15] Shakyamuni attained to Buddhahood, and there were many who saw him, yet they did not behold in him the Buddha; while now, after he has entered into Paranirvana, there are many who never saw him in the body, yet having attained faith may truly be said to behold the Buddha, for the Buddha can be recognised with the mind's eye alone."[16]

"Then Amitâbha is the principle of being as much as Brahma?" enquired Charaka.

"Brahma is a personification of the principle of being," replied Açvaghosha, "but Amitâbha is the standard of being. Amitâbha is the intrinsic law which, whenever being rises into existence, moulds life and develops it, producing uniformities and regularities in both the world of realities and the realm of thought. It is the source of rationality and righteousness, of science and of morality, of philosophy and religion. The sage of the Shakyas is one ray of its light only, albeit for us the most powerful ray, with the clearest, brightest, and purest light. He is the light that came to us here in this world and in our country. Wheresoever wisdom appears, there is an incarnation, more or less partial, more or less complete, of Amitâbha."

"But existence," rejoined Charaka, "is different from the good law. Being is one thing and the norm that moulds it another. There is the great question, whether or not life itself is wrong. If life is wrong, the joy of living is sin, the enhancement of life, including its reproduction, an error, and love, the love of husband and wife, becomes a just cause for repentance."

"Mark the doctrine, noble youth, and act accordingly," replied Açvaghosha. "I read in your eyes the secret of your heart which prompts you to ask this question. Goodness is a reality which exists in both existence and non-existence. Call it God or Amitâbha, or Allhood, or the eternal and uncreated, the universal law, the not-bodily, the nothing or non-existence, for it is not concrete nor material, nor real to the senses,—yet it exists, it is spiritual and can be discovered by the mind; it is and remains for all that exists the intrinsic and necessary norm; it is the rule and regulation for both things and thoughts. It is omnipresent in the universe, invisible, impalpable, as a perfume that permeates a room. Whatever makes its appearance as a concrete reality is affected by its savor and nothing can be withdrawn from its sway. It is not existence itself, but the womb of existence; it is that which gives definite shape to beings, moulding them and determining them according to conditions. You have Amitâbha in two aspects as the formation of particular existence and as the general law of universal types. The particular is the realisation of the universal; and the universal constitutes the type of the particular, giving it a definite character. Neither is without the other. Mere particularity is being in a state of ignorance; thus all life starts in ignorance; but mere universality is existence unrealised; it is as though existence were not. Therefore enjoyment of life is not wrong and the love of husband and wife is no cause for repentance, if it be but the right love, true and unfailing and making each willing to bear the burdens of the other.

"The Lord spoke not of God, because the good law that becomes incarnated in Buddhahood is not a somebody, not an entity, not an ego, not even a ghost. As there is not a ghost-soul, so there is not a ghost-God."

Said Charaka: "Now I understand the picture of the Lord Buddha with his two attendants, Love as Particularity on the elephant and Wisdom as Universality on the lion. Ananda, the disciple of loving service, and Kâshyapa, the disciple of philosophical intellectuality, have approached their master and grasped the significance of his doctrine from two opposite and contrasting sides."

"Those who mortify their bodies," continued Açvaghosha, "have not understood the doctrine. We are not ego-souls. For that reason the thought of an individual escape, the salvation of our ego-soul, is a heresy and an illusion. We all stand together and every man must work for the salvation of mankind. Therefore I love to compare the doctrine of the Buddha to a great ship or a grand vehicle

—a Mahâyâna—in which there is room for all the multitudes of living beings and we who stand at the helm must save them all or perish with them."

Charaka extended his hand and said: "I thank you, venerable sir, for the light you have afforded me. I sought peace of soul in a monastery, but the love of life, the love of God, the love of knowledge, the love of my heart, drove me back to the world. I have proved useful to King Kanishka as a physician, perhaps also as a friend, and as a disciple of the Tathâgata; and the problem before me is, whether it is right for me to remain in the world, to be a householder, to allow the particular, the sensual, the actual, a share in life by the side of the universal, the spiritual, the ideal."

"Do not despise the particular, the sensual, the actual," replied Açvaghosha. "In the material body the spiritual truths of goodness and love and veracity are actualised. Existence if it is mere existence, quantity of life and not quality, is worthless and contemptible. The sage despises it. The sensual, if it be void of the spiritual, is coarse and marks the brute. But existence is not wrong in itself, nor is the sensual without its good uses. The sensual, in its very particularity, by being an aspiration that is actual, becomes consecrated in spirituality. Think how holy is the kiss of true love; how sacred is the relation between husband and wife. It is the particular in which the universal must be realised, mere abstract goodness will become apparent only in the vicissitudes of actual life."

"If I could serve the Buddha as a householder, my highest ambition would be to be a brother-in-law to King Kanishka," replied Charaka.

"I know it," said Açvaghosha with a smile, "for the emotions of your heart are reflected in your eyes. Go home and greet the king's sister with a saying of the Blessed One, and when you are married may your happiness be in proportion to your merit, or even greater and better. Buddha's doctrine is not extinction, not nihilism, but a liberation of man's heart from the fetters of selfishness and from the seclusion of a separate egoity. It is not the suppression or eradication of love, and joy, and family ties, but their perfection and sanctification; not a cessation of life, but a cessation of ignorance, indolence, and ill will, for the sake of gaining enlightenment, which is life's end and aim."

After a pause Açvaghosha added pensively: "The more the truth spreads, the more shall all relations and conditions be transfigured by Buddhahood. Even the dumb creatures and inanimate nature are yearning for their emancipation that is to come."

"Your instruction has benefited me too," said Kanishka to the philosopher, and turning round to the king of Magadha, he continued, "but you my noble friend and host are still my debtor. Since Açvaghosha on account of his age finds himself unable to follow me to Gandhâra, you are in duty bound to procure an acceptable substitute. Now, there is a way of settling your obligations to me, and that could be done if your daughter, the Princess Bhadraçrî would consent to accept my hand and accompany me to Gandhâra as my wife and queen!"

"My august friend," replied the king of Magadha, "I know that the Princess worships you for the heroism you have displayed in battle, the wisdom you have shown in council, and the magnanimity with which you have dealt with your conquered enemy. She beholds in you not only the ideal of royalty but also the restorer of her father's fortunes, worthy of her sincerest gratitude. It is but for you to make her admiration blossom out into rich love and wifely devotion."

THE CONSPIRACY.

ACVAGHOSHA held daily conversations with Kanishka, in which not only his friends Charaka and the king of Magadha, but also Princess Bhadraçrî, his bride-elect, were now wont to join.

One day Subâhu was detained by important affairs of state, and when he made his appearance in the accustomed circle of his philosophical friends, he was so full of distress as to be almost beyond the power of speech.

"My royal friend," said Kanishka, "what disturbs your mind? How terrible must the calamity be that so affects a man of your composure! Are you or one of your kin in danger of death, or pray, what else is the cause of your trouble?"

"My dear friend and ally," replied king Subâhu, "it is your life that is endangered. I come to take counsel with you as to how we may save you from the perilous situation in which the false patriotism of my people has placed you. Some of my southern generals having but lately arrived with subsidies which ought to have been with me at the beginning of the war, entered into a conspiracy with my prime minister to surround the palace, take you prisoner and put you to the sword; then to attack your unwary soldiers and drive them out of the country. Everything has been planned in the strictest privacy, and your noble confidence in my faith and friendship made it easy for them to replace the guards gradually by their friends until they now have everything their own way, and I am given to undersand that unless I join the conspirators they will elect another king."

"And what is your pleasure in this matter?" asked Kanishka, who betrayed no more concern than if he were talking about a game of checkers.

"My pleasure?" exclaimed the disconsolate king; "ask not what my pleasure is. I see only my duty, and that is to save you or to die with you!"

Kanishka was a man of deeds, not of words. He bade Charaka at once to hoist on the tower of the palace a blue flag, which was the secret sign to summon the Gandhâra generals that were camping in the vicinity of the town. Having inquired into the situation and learned that all the gates were in possession of the conspirators, he requested the king to call into his presence the treacherous prime minister who was at the head of the conspiracy, indicating, as though nothing had happened, that he wanted to speak to him.

The prime minister entered, and the king spoke to him graciously about his fidelity to King Subâhu and the kingdom of Magadha, and said that he himself, anxious to honor the people of Magadha, wished to show him some recognition and confer some favor on him, the most faithful servant of King Subâhu.

While King Kanishka thus idled away the time the prime minister felt uneasy, for his fellow-conspirators, the generals from the south, were waiting for the signal to overpower the few foreign guards, to close the gates, and take possession of the palace. Kanishka in the meanwhile inquired as to his health, his general prosperity, his children, his brothers and sisters, until the prime minister lost patience and said: "Sire, allow me to withdraw; a number of my friends from the southern provinces, men of great prominence in their distant homes, have arrived and are anxious to meet me and my sovereign."

With a royal courtesy which could not be refused, King Kanishka replied: "Let me accompany you to greet them. Your friends are my friends, and the vassals of my most noble ally King Subâhu are my allies."

The prime minister blushed and looked inquiringly at the king; but King Kanishka's eye was calm and showed not the least sign of suspicion. At the same time there was a firmness and determination in the king's attitude which made the treacherous minister wince and submit.

"This is the way to the hall where my friends are assembled," said the prime minister, and showed the king the way.

"Wait a moment," said King Kanishka, "it would be wrong of us if my royal brother, King

Subâhu, were not present. Let us call my councilors and generals so as to indicate our desire to honor your guests."

In the meantime some of the horsemen had arrived, and their officers demanded admission at the palace gates to report their presence to the king. They were announced and admitted.

"Welcome, my gallant officers," exclaimed King Kanishka, "join my retinue when I greet the friends of the prime minister, and let your men remain under arms at the main gate ready to receive my commands."

Thus the two kings with a stately retinue both of dignified councilors and warlike officers entered the hall where the conspirators were impatiently waiting. They were dumbfounded when they saw at the side of their most hated enemy their own sovereign accompanied by the prime minister with downcast eye, meek as a tame doe and giving no sign for action. Then Kanishka addressed the conspirators with great cordiality as though he had long desired to meet them and show them his good will. He praised the generals for their valor, for their love of their country, their faithfulness to their king, and expressed his great happiness that the old times of national hatred had passed away, that the two nations Magadha and Gandhâra should forthwith be like brothers, and that they would join to set a good example to the world by obeying the maxim of the Tathâgata:

> "Hate is not overcome by hate;
> By love alone 'tis quelled.
> This is a truth of ancient date,
> To-day still unexcelled."[17]

Not yet, however, had the ice of spite and ill will entirely melted from the hostile hearts of his enemies; and not yet was his retinue strong enough to make him feel master of the situation. So Kanishka continued his policy of gaining time by having each one of the hostile officers personally introduced to him and, this done, he began to address the company a second time.

"Allow me to improve this rare opportunity of having so many friends assembled here, to explain my policy. I am a disciple of the Buddha, the Blessed One, who taught us to make an end of hatred by ceasing to hate. If there be any just cause for war, let us have war and let us wage war openly and resolutely, but let us ever be ready to offer the hand of brotherly good-will to our enemies without cherishing feelings of revenge for the injuries we may think we have suffered. The policy of long suffering, of loving-kindness, of forgiveness, not only shows goodness of heart but also a rare gift of wisdom, as all those are aware who know the story of King Long-suffering and his noble son Prince Long-life, which the Tathâgata told to the quarrelsome monks of Kaushâmbî.

King Kanishka then told the story of Brahmadatta, the powerful king of Benares,—how he had conquered the little kingdom of Kôsala and had the captive king Long-suffering executed in Benares. But Prince Long-life escaped and, unknown to any one, entered the service of King Brahmadatta, whose confidence he gained by his talents and reliability. Thus be became King Brahmadatta's personal attendant.

King Kanishka was a good story-teller, and

the people of India, whether of high or low birth, love to hear a story well told, even if they know it by heart. So the conspirators were as though spellbound and forgot their evil designs; nor did they notice how the hall began to fill more and more with the officers of the king of Gandhâra. They listened to the adventures of Prince Long-life; how on a hunt he was left alone with King Brahmadatta in the forest, how the king laid himself down and slept, how the prince drew his sword, how the king was frightened when he awoke and learned that he was in the power of his enemy's son; and finally how each granted the other his life and made peace, thus demonstrating the wisdom of the maxim, that hatred cannot be appeased by hatred, but is appeased by love, —and by love only.[18]

When the king finished the story of Prince Long-life, the hall was crowded with armed officers of the Gandhâra army, and seeing his advantage, King Kanishka, feeling the satisfaction of one who had gained a great victory in battle, paused and glanced with a good-natured look over the party of conspirators.

He remained as self-possessed as a schoolmaster teaching a class of wayward boys. "I am anxious to be at peace with all the world," he said, "but the question arises, what shall be done with traitors and conspirators who misunderstand my good intentions and would not brook the loving-kindness of our great master?" Then addressing the prime minister of Magadha by his full name and title, he added: "Let me hear your advice, my friend. I meant to promote your welfare, while you attempted to take my life. What shall I do with you and your associates?"

The prime minister was overwhelmed. He fell upon his knees and sobbed: "You are in wisdom like the Enlightened One, the Omniscient Tathâgata. Would that you were his equal also in mercy and compassion. Never should you regret having forgiven me my transgression!"

King Kanishka made no answer but looked round and cast conquering glances at the several conspirators, until they, one by one, joined the kneeling prime minister. Then espying the venerable head of Açvaghosha among his audience, he approached the sage respectfully and said: "Now, most reverend sir, it is your turn to speak, for I want you to tell me what a king ought to do to those men who conspire to take his life. Would it be wise for him to follow the behest of the Tathâgata and to grant them forgiveness?"

Said Açvaghosha: "Not I, sir, but you are the king. Pronounce judgment according to your own discretion. I cherish the confidence that the seeds of kindness will fall here upon good soil."

"Thank you, venerable sir. I have learned from the Great Teacher of all beings, that to hate no one is the highest wisdom. But a king is responsible for the welfare of his people and cannot let crime go unpunished. The duty of a judge is justice. In the present case I do not think that I would condone your action if it were unmitigated treason but I see in it a redeeming feature which is your patriotism, misguided though it may be. Rise, gentlemen, and if you will promise forthwith to banish from your heart all falsehood, spite, and envy, come and shake hands with me in token of your faithful allegiance to both your august sovereign, the king of Magadha, and myself, his ally and brother on the throne."

THE MAN-EATING TIGER.

PROTESTATIONS of fidelity and admiration greeted King Kanishka from all sides when he retired to his private rooms after having shaken hands with the conspirators. He had conquered his enemies, not by the power of arms, as he had done before in battle, but by the superiority of his mind.

It was at this moment that a messenger arrived who had been sent by the custodian of King Subâhu's summer palace, saying: "Sir King, send your hunters to the summer palace with elephants and soldiers, for a man-eating tiger has been seen in its garden and parks, and all the people living in the neighborhood are sore afraid of the beast."

Then the generals of the South shouted: "Great King and Sire, allow us to go to the summer palace to hunt the tiger; for we are anxious to distinguish ourselves and prove to the world that we are valiant soldiers and good hunters."

And they received permission to be the foremost in the hunt, and after a hasty preparation they set out the same evening, but the two kings and their retinue with many officers followed them on the following day; Charaka, however, stayed behind at the command of King Kanishka, to observe the courtiers and councilors of King Subâhu and keep an eye upon the populace of the city, the capital of Magadha.

Charaka sat at a window in company with the venerable Açvaghosha to see the suite of the two kings with their hunters and elephants leaving the city, and Charaka addressed the sage, saying: "My reverend friend, I learned much yesterday from king Kanishka by watching his mode of treating enemies. Truly, I understand the doctrine of the Tathâgata better now than if I had lived for many years in the monastery and studied all the wisdom of the monks. How much evil can be avoided by discretion, and should not mortals blame themselves for all the ills that befall them?

But there is this doubt that vexes my mind. If Amitâbha, the omnipresent, the eternal, the omnibeneficent source of all wisdom, fashions the world and determines our destinies, why should not life be possible without suffering? However, the first sentence of the four great truths declares that life itself is suffering. If that be so, no amount of discretion could give us happiness so long as we live. And, on the other hand, how can Amitâbha permit innumerable things to suffer innocently for conditions which they did not create themselves?"

"My young friend," replied Açvaghosha, "the first great truth is truly obvious to any one who knows the nature of life. Life consists of separation and combination; it is a constant meeting and parting and has in store both pains and pleasures. Prove to me that life be possible without any change, and I will begin to doubt the first of the four great truths. But if life is suffering, no being has a right to blame Amitâbha for existing. All beings exist by their own karma; they are the incarnation of deeds of their former existences; they are such as they are by their own determination, having fashioned themselves under the influence of circumstances.

"By Amitâbha all beings are merely educated in the school of life. Some have gained more insight than others. Some love the light, others hate it. Some rise to the pure heights of Buddhahood, and others grovel in the dust to take delight in badness and deeds of darkness. Amitâbha is like the rain that falls upon the earth without discrimination. The seeds of herbs assimilate the water that falls from the clouds of heaven in a refreshing spring shower, and grow to be herbs each of its kind. Fernspores become ferns, acorns change the water into the leaves and wood and bark of oak trees, and the germs of fruit trees fashion it into fruit, each of its own kind, into mangoes, bananas, dates, figs, pomegranates, and other savory fruits. Amitâbha is the same to all, as the water of the refreshing rain is the same: but diverse creatures make a different use of the benefits of truth, and each one is responsible for itself.[19] Each one has originated in ignorance by its own blind impulses, each one, in its own field of experience, has learned the lesson of life in its own way, and each one can blame no one but itself for what it is and has become—except that it ought to be grateful for the light that Amitâbha sheds upon the course of its development.

"Amitâbha is not a god that would assert himself or care for worship and adoration. He does not think and act and do deeds. He is not Ishvara, not Sakra, not Indra, not Brahma: He is the norm of all existence, the good law, the order and intrinsic harmony that shows itself in cause and effect, in the bliss of goodness, in the curse of evil-doing. He is above all the gods, and everything that is has been fashioned by him according to the eternal ordinances of his constitution.

"We are not creatures of Amitâbha, we are creatures of our own making. Life starts in ignorance. It begins with blind impulses, and life's start is life's own doing. But as soon as an impulse acts and is reacted upon, it is encompassed by the good law and thus it is educated by Amitâbha and raised by him as children are nourished by their mother and instructed by their father. We are not the creatures of Amitâbha, but his children.[20]

"Ask thy own self, whether thou art because thou wast created by some extraneous power; or contrariwise whether it is not truer to say that thou art because thou dost will thy own existence. Every man is what he wills to be.

"Thou hast become what thou art of necessity according to the norms that constitute the nature of Amitâbha. But thou grewest to be what thou art because thou wantedst to become such.

"Now if an Ishvara had created thee, thou wouldst not have the feeling of freedom that thou now hast, but thou wouldst feel like the vessel made by the potter which is what it is in spite of its own like or dislike."

"But if I am determined to love life," asked Charaka, "is it wrong to do so and shall I be punished for it by suffering?"

Replied Açvaghosha: "There is neither punishment nor reward, my son, though we may use the words in adapting our language to the common mode of thought. There is only cause and effect. The Tathâgata gave no commandments, for what authority has any one to command his brother beings? The Tathâgata revealed to us the evils of life, and what people call the ten commandments are the ten ways pointed out by the Tathâgata how to avoid the ten evils. He who does not take the Tathâgata's advice must bear the consequences. The tiger will be hunted down, and a murderer will be executed. Their fate is the result of their deeds. As to love of life, there is nothing wrong in it. If you love life, you must not be afraid of suffering. While the Tathâgata lived in the flesh, he was as much subject to pain as I am and as you are. But when the pangs of his last disease came upon him he bore them with fortitude and did not complain. If you love life, bear its ills nobly and do not break down under its burdens. Avail yourself of the light of Amitâbha, for thus you can escape the worst evils of life, the contrition of regret, of remorse, of a bad conscience; and the noblest pleasure of life is that of becoming a lamp unto others. Let your light shine in the world and you will be like unto your master, Buddha-Amitâbha, the omnibenevolent source of all illumination."

THE BUDDHIST ABBOT AND THE BRAHMAN.

WHILE King Kanishka stayed at the summer palace to witness the tiger hunt, a Buddhist abbot came to the royal palace and requested an interview with the great King Kanishka's friend; and the abbot was admitted into the presence of Charaka, who happened to be in the company of some councilors of King Subâhu, among whom was Açvaghosha, the saintly philosopher. Said the abbot: "I come from the monastery in the hills situated near a Brahman village south of Benares and have been sent by the brethren, the venerable monks whose abbot I am. We know that King Kanishka and you are followers of the Buddha and are steadfast in the orthodox faith. Therefore we approach you in confidence and hope that you will lend your countenance to us, endeavoring to spread and establish the good law, the pure religion of the Tathâgata. We have settled in the hills, but there is a Shiva shrine close by and the villagers continue to offer gifts to the priests while the venerable brethren who profess faith in the glorious doctrine of the Buddha are neglected and sometimes positively suffer from privation."

"What can I do about it?" queried Charaka.

"If the Shiva shrine were removed, the villagers would no longer seek religious comfort through Brahman rites and would turn Buddhists. We are told that you are a Buddhist monk; you will have sympathy with your suffering brethren and help them to expel the unbelievers."

"And do you think," objected Açvaghosha, "that either King Subâhu or King Kanishka would lend you his royal authority to interfere with the religious service of any one? No, my friend. The Shiva worshipers may be mistaken in their religious views, but they seek the truth and so long as they do no injury to their neighbors, their worship cannot be disturbed. And I do not know but the Shiva priests may in their own way do good service to the people."

And there was a Brahman present, one of King Subâhu's councilors, who was pleased with Açvaghosha's remark and expressed his approval of the principle of toleration which the great emperor Açoka had proclaimed in one of his edicts as a maxim of good government, and the Brahman added:

"Do not ye, too, O Buddhists, preach the doctrine of the Brahmans, that there is a supreme Lord Creator over all creatures, a divine ego-consciousness of All-existence? Whether we call God Ishvara, or Shiva, or Amitâbha, he remains the same and has a just claim to worship."

Açvaghosha shook his head: "No, my Brahman friend! The good law is supreme, and it is a father omnibenevolent as we rightly designate it. It is the norm of existence, the standard of truth, the measure of righteousness; but that norm is not an Ishvara, neither Shiva, nor Brahma. Here is the difference between Ishvara and Amitâbha: Ishvara is deified egotism; he demands worship and praise. Amitâbha is love, he is free from the vanity of egoism and is only anxious for his children that they should avail themselves of the light and shun the darkness, that they should follow his advice and walk in the path of righteousness. Ishvara calls sin what is contrary to his will; he loves to be addressed in prayer and he delights in listening to the praises of his worshipers. Not so Amitâbha. Amitâbha cares not for prayer, is indifferent to worship, and cannot be flattered by praise, but the good law is thwarted when his children err; and Amitâbha appears to be wrapt in sadness by the evil results of their mistakes; not for his sake—for he is eternal and remains the same forevermore—but for the sake of the sufferings of all sentient creatures, for all creatures are his disciples, he guides them, he teaches them, he encompasses them. He is like a father unto them. So far as they partake of his nature, they are his children."

Said the Brahman: "I for one do not believe that Ishvara, or Brahma, or whatever you may call God, is a person such as we are. He is a higher kind of personality, which however includes the faculties of perception, judgment and reason. I believe therefore that the Buddhist faith is lacking in this, that its devotees think of Amitâbha as deficient in self-consciousness. Buddhist ethics are noble, but are human deeds the highest imaginable? Since the godhead is greater than man, the highest bliss will forever remain a union with Brahma, or Ishvara, or Sakra, or whatever you may call the great Unknown and Unknowable, who has revealed himself in the Vedas and is pleased with the prayers and sacrifices of the pious who express their faith in worship."

"When I was young," replied Açvaghosha, "I was a Brahman myself; I believed in Brahma the Supreme Being, the Creator of and Lord over all the worlds that exist. I know there is much that is good in the Brahman faith, and I did not abandon it because I deemed it bad or injurious. I abandoned it, because the doctrine of the Tathâgata was superior, all-comprehensive, and more profound, for it explains the problems of existence, its whence and whither, and is more helpful. The doctrine of the Tathâgata is practical and not in the air as are the theories and speculations of the Brahmans. You seek a union with Brahma, and what is he? We may dispute his existence and no one can refute us. He is an idea, a metaphysical assumption, and his mansion is everywhere and nowhere. Thus the Tathâgata says that those who believe in Brahma are like a man who should make a staircase where four roads meet, to mount up high into a mansion which he can neither see nor know how it is, where it is, what it is built of, nor whether it exists at all. The priests claim the authority of the Vedas, and the Vedas are based upon the authority of the authors who wrote them, and these authors rely on the authority of Brahma. They are like a string of blind men clinging to one another and leading the blind, and their method of salvation consists in adoration, worship, and prayer.[21] It is a doctrine for children, and though the words of their theory are high-sounding they are not the truth but a mere shadow of the truth; and in this sense the Tathâgata compared them to the monkey at the lake who tries to catch the moon in the water, mistaking the reflection for the reality."

"But would not all your arguments," replied the Brahman, "if I were to grant them, apply with the same force to Amitâbha? What is the difference whether we say Brahma or Amitâbha? Both are names for the Absolute.".

"There would be no difference in the names if we understood the same by both. Brahma, the Absolute, is generally interpreted to mean Being in general, but Amitâbha is Enlightenment. We do not hanker after existence, but we worship truth, goodness, and purity.

"By Amitâbha we understand the eternal, infinite light, i. e., the spiritual light of comprehension, and this light is a reality. No one doubts that there is a norm of truth and a standard of right and wrong. That is Amitâbha. We may not yet know all about Amitâbha; our wisdom is limited; our goodness is not perfect. But we ground ourselves upon that which we do know, while you Brahmans start with speculations, seeking a union with the Absolute, which is a vague idea, something unknown and unknowable. Amitâbha is certainly not a limited self-consciousness, but an infinite principle, an omnipresent law, an eternal norm, higher than any individual, but the depth of this norm is unfathomable, its application universal and infinite; its bountiful use immeasurable.

"We know something but not all about Amitâbha. He is the Dharmakâya, the embodiment of the good law. He is the Nirmanakâya, the aspiration to reach bodhi in the transformations of the evolution of life. He is the Sambhogakâya, the bliss of good deeds.[22] The philosophers, scientists, poets, of the future, the thinkers and dreamers of mankind, will find in Amitâbha a wonderful source of inspiration which can never be exhausted. The Tathâgata's religion is not mere metaphysics, his philosophy is not mere mythology. He allows metaphysics and mythology their spheres, but urges the practical issues of life. Thus his religion comprises all without becoming vague."

Said the Brahman: "How can so many contradictory things be united in one?"

And Açvaghosha replied: "My venerable

teacher, the saintly sage Parsva, once told me the parable of the elephant which explains the relation of the truth to the sundry doctrines held by the several sects and schools, priests and philosophers, prophets and preachers.

The Brahman said that he had never heard the story, and expressed his desire to hear it.

THE PARABLE OF THE ELEPHANT.

ACVAGHOSHA saw that every eye was intent upon him, and so he told the story of the white Elephant. He said:

"There was a noble and mighty elephant, an elephant white in color, with a strong trunk and long tusks, trained by a good master, and willing and serviceable in all the work that elephants are put to. And this noble and mighty elephant being led by his guide, the good master who had trained him, came to the land of the blind. And it was noised about in the land of the blind that the noble and mighty elephant, the king of all beasts, the wisest of all animals, the strongest and yet the meekest and kindliest of creatures, had made his appearance in their country. So the wise men and teachers of the blind came to the place where the elephant was and every one began to investigate his shape and figure and form. And when the elephant was gone they met and discussed the problem of the noble and mighty beast, and there were some who said he was like a great thick snake; others said he was like a snake of medium size. The former had felt the trunk, the latter the tail. Further there were some who claimed that his figure was like that of a high column, others declared he was large and bulky like a big barrel, still others maintained he was smooth and hard but tapering. Some of the blind had taken hold of one of the legs, others had reached the main body, and still others had touched the tusks. Every one proposed his view and they disputed and controverted, and wrangled, and litigated, and bickered, and quarreled, and called each other names, and each one imprecated all the others, and each one denounced all the others, and they abused and scolded, and they anathematised and excommunicated, and finally every one of them swore that every one else was a liar and was cursed on account of his heresies. These blind men, every one of them honest in his contentions, being sure of having the truth and relying upon his own experience, formed schools and sects and factions and behaved in exactly the same way as you see the priests of the different creeds behave. But the master of the noble, mighty elephant knows them all, he knows that every one of them has a parcel of the truth, that every one is right in his way, but wrong in taking his parcel to be the whole truth.

"Not one of these sectarians observed the fact that the elephant was perfectly white and a marvel to see, for all of them were purblind. Yet I would not say that they were either dishonest or hypocrites. They had investigated the truth to the best of their ability.

"The master of the elephant is the Tathâgata, the Enlightened One, the Buddha. He has brought the white elephant representing the truth, the noble and mighty elephant, symbolising strength and wisdom and devotion, into the land of the blind, and he who listens to the Tathâgata will understand all the schools, and all the sects and all the factions that are in possession of parcels of the truth. His doctrine is all-comprehensive, and he who takes refuge in Him will cease to bicker, and to contend, and to quarrel."[23]

* * *

When Açvaghosha had finished the parable of the noble and mighty elephant, the two kings returned from the summer palace carrying with them in a solemn procession the slain tiger, and close behind on a white charger decked with garlands and gay ribbons, rode the hero of the day, one of the generals from the South, whose dart had struck the tiger with fatal precision and death-dealing power.

"Behold the hero of the day!" said Charaka. "And had the conspiracy not miscarried the same man might now be an assassin and a miscreant."

"There is a lesson in it!" replied Açvaghosha, "existence is not desirable for its own sake. That which gives worth to life is the purpose to which it is devoted.

"Our aim is not to live, but whether we die or live, to avoid wrong doing and to let right and justice and lovingkindness prevail. Says the Tathâgata:

"Commit no wrong, but good deeds do,
And let thy heart be pure.
All Buddhas teach this doctrine true
Which will for aye endure."[24]

THE DOUBLE WEDDING.

CHARAKA found by degrees and not without difficulties his mental equilibrium, which his friend Kanishka seemed to possess naturally. He unburdened his heart to the saintly old man and arrived at the conviction that he was not made for a monk and that his duties of life according to his disposition lay in other fields.

In the meantime King Kanishka had sent a messenger to Matura his chancellor and vicegerent at Gandhâra, to bring Princess Kamalavatî to Benares.

Princess Kamalavatî arrived, and when her betrothal to Charaka was announced the happy events of our story reached their climax. Açvaghosha solemnised the nuptials of both couples, Kanishka with Bhadraçrî, and Charaka with Kamalavatî; and he read to them from the Dhammapada the famous stanza:

"Sweet in the world is fatherhood,
And motherhood is sweet;
But sweeter is the thought of good,
If nobly our heart beat.

"Sweeter, a life to old age spent
In truth and purity;
Sweeter, to reach enlightenment
And keep from evil free."[25]

When the marriage ceremony was over a feast was spread at the royal palace, and King Kanishka declared that he had a great respect for priests, but did not favor the idea that his friend, the physician royal, should resign his calling of wizard (as he was wont to call him) for the sake of becoming a monk. While there were plenty of good and honest men to wear the yellow robe, there was scarcely one man among a million who could perform miracles and save human lives, as Charaka had done.

Charaka denied that he was a wizard. His art was no magic but consisted simply in observation and experiment, and it was nature whose forces he had learned to guide; but for all that he accomplished things which astounded the world. They were better than the miracles of magicians, for they were more useful and of enduring benefit to mankind.

When his friends praised him, he replied: "My science is a beginning only and what I accomplish is the work of a tyro. The Tathâgata has preached the religion of enlightenment, he set the wheel rolling; it is now our duty to follow up his thought, to spread enlightenment, and to increase it. Amitâbha is infinite, and thus the possibilities of invention are inexhaustible. The wondrous things which man is able to do, and which he will do in the ages to come, can at present only be surmised by the wisest sages.

"But greater than the greatest feats of invention will be the application of the Lord Buddha's maxim of loving-kindness in all fields of human intercourse, in family life, in politics, in labor and social affairs, in our dealings with friends and foes, with animals, and even with the degenerate and criminal. The enlightenment of our souls is most important. Therefore we praise the Tathâgata above all other things.

"Bright shineth the sun in his splendor by day
And bright the moon's radiance by night,
Bright shineth the hero in battle array,
And the sage in his thought shineth bright.
But by day and by night, none so glorious so bright
As Lord Buddha, the source of all spiritual light."

NOTES.

Page 1.

[1] For details of the pabbajja (or initiation) and the upasampada (or ordination) see *Mahâvagga,* first khandaka (*S. B. E.,* Val. XIII).

Page 3.

[2] The time of our story is the fifth century after the Buddha's enlightenment, which corresponds to the first century of the Christian era.

Page 6.

[3] Cf. "Buddhist Chants and Processions," *Journal of the Buddhist Text Society of India,* Vol. III, Part II.

Page 10.

[4] Dhammapada, 21.

[5] Dhammapada, 223.

Page 11.

[6] Dhammapada, 134.

[7] Dhammapada, 313.

[8] Dhammapada, 258; 240.

Page 12.

[9] Dhammapada, 254.

Page 31.

[10] Kevaddha's story is an abbreviated account of an ancient Buddhist Pali text. The verses as well as other details are almost literally translated. Cf. Henry Warren's *Buddhism in Translations,* pp. 308-313.